You're the
Butter
on My
Biscuit!

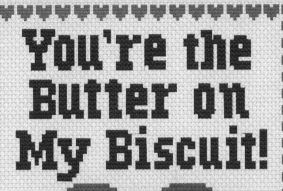

You're the Butter on My Biscuit!

And Other Country Sayin's 'bout Love, Marriage, and Heartache

Allan Zullo and **Gene Cheek**

Andrews McMeel
Publishing, LLC

Kansas City · Sydney · London

For information, write Andrews McMeel Publishing, LLC,
an Andrews McMeel Universal company, 1130 Walnut Street,
Kansas City, Missouri 64106.

10 11 12 13 14 MLT 10 9 8 7 6 5 4 3 2 1

ISBN: 978-0-7407-9754-5

Library of Congress Control Number: 2010924516

www.andrewsmcmeel.com

Attention: Schools and Businesses
Andrews McMeel books are available at quantity discounts
with bulk purchase for educational, business, or
sales promotional use. For information, please write to:
Special Sales Department, Andrews McMeel Publishing, LLC,
1130 Walnut Street, Kansas City, Missouri 64106.

To the gal I married during the Summer of Love. Kathy, it's always summer with you.
—A.Z.

♥ ♥ ♥

From family to friends, I have had more than my share of remarkable people in my life. I have loved them all, and fortunately, some of them have loved me back. This book is dedicated to them.
—G.C.

Contents

Gooder 'n Snuff

While collecting country sayings for our book *Butter My Butt and Call Me a Biscuit* and for our calendar series of the same name, we couldn't help but notice that the down-home people of the farms, mountains, and ranges of America have had plenty to say about love, marriage, breakups, and heartache.

Yes, some of these say-sos are more corny and cheesy than corn fritters and cheese grits, but there's almost always an element of truth in these beliefs from the nation's backwoods and front porches, reflecting a way of thinking that can touch us all in different ways. When it comes to what love is and isn't, country folk paint their sentences in the most vivid and original analogies, sew simple words of emotion together into quilts of truisms, and season their language with zesty wit and biting rage.

So it was as natural as a mess of skinny-dippers on a hot summer day for us to gather a whole new bunch of notions, musings, and look-sees for the lovesick and lovelorn and put them in a second book.

This fresh collection of old-timey phrases, metaphors, and axioms is designed to tickle your funny bone one moment and tug at your heartstrings the next. If you've been smitten by Cupid, you'll find country love sayings that are as tender and sweet as honey-dipped chicken wings. You'll see for yourself that when it comes to romance, the denizens of the hollows, hamlets, and hinterlands of America have their own charming, inventive ways of speaking from the heart.

But heaven help you if you cross them, because there's another side to country talk—a furious flurry of poison-tipped barbs aimed at cheaters, ne'er-do-wells, and cads who have broken lovers' hearts. If you're suffering from heartache or you're seeking revenge over a romance that turned sour, you'll find plenty of boonies-born sayings that are as fiery and spicy as chile peppers dipped in homemade horseradish.

The sayings have emerged from virtually every nook and cranny of America—in lovey-dovey places like Romance, Arkansas; Sweet Lips, Tennessee; Bridal Veil, Oregon; Matrimony, North Carolina; Valentine, Nebraska; Loving, Oklahoma; and Hearts Content, Pennsylvania, as well as anguished-sounding places like Bitter End, Tennessee; Screamersville, Virginia; Hell Hollow, New Hampshire; Bedlam, Connecticut; Loveless, Alabama; Heartease, Mississippi; Little Hope, Texas; and Farewell, Missouri.

We have a deep appreciation for rural expressions, having lived in North Carolina's Blue Ridge Mountains for years—Gene is a born-and-bred Tar Heel; Allan and his wife, Kathryn, moved to the Ol' North State in 1995. For *You're the Butter on My Biscuit!*, we collected hundreds of delightfully clever and colorful sayings about love. We also included dozens of country jokes and the titles of real country songs that have captured the joy of spoonin', courtin', gettin' hitched, and havin' relations as well as the sorrow and rage of gettin' ditched and gettin' even. We chose to end the book with a chapter chock full of down-home wisdom about love in one-liners that are just as insightful today as when they were first spoken decades ago.

Whether you're looking for countrified advice, country-style ways to say, "I love you," backwoods put-downs for ex-sweethearts, or hee-haw laughs about dating and marriage, you should find plenty that you'll love to repeat to your sweetie pie or your ex.

We hope the sayings prove to be as delightful as okra fryin' in the pan . . . and gooder 'n snuff right out of the can.

—Allan Zullo and Gene Cheek

SPARKIN' AN' SPOONIN'

(Notions 'bout Datin')

Fun

If you're telling someone about the great evening you had with your date at the dance, you might say . . .

We had ourselves a hog-killin' time.

Anticipation

To someone wondering how an upcoming date will turn out, you might say . . .

You can never tell which way the pickle's gonna squirt.

2

Charisma

- - - - - - - -

Speaking about a guy who swept
a girl off her feet with a romantic
gesture, you might say . . .

He sure bowled that maiden over.

Anxiety

- - - - - - - -

If you're going out on a highly
anticipated date for the first time,
you might say . . .

*I'm as nervous as a mama cow
with a bucktoothed calf.*

Competition
- - - - - - - - -

In advising a really nice guy
who's wondering if he should
compete against a stud athlete
for the attentions of a gal,
you might say . . .

If you can't sing, dance.

Hearsay
- - - - - - - - -

If you're hearing wild rumors
about a girl you want to date,
you might say . . .

*Them's the kinda things a fella likes
to find out for himself.*

4

Some Surprise

A country boy walks up to the perfume counter at Woolworth's and tells the clerk he'd like a bottle of perfume for his girlfriend's birthday.

The clerk smiles and says, "You're gonna surprise her, huh?"

"Yep," he answers. "She's expectin' a diamond ring."

Knowledge

- - - - - - - - -

To a girl who's agreed to go out
with a fellow she knows nothing
about, you might say . . .

*Never test the depth of the water
with both feet.*

Rejection

- - - - - - - - -

To someone who turned down a
date with a good-looking nice guy,
you might say . . .

*The piece of pie you pass up is the piece
you'll never get.*

Yearning

- - - - - - - - -

If you have a strong desire or
longing to ask out a certain girl,
you might say . . .

I've got a hankerin' to call on her.

Risk

- - - - - - - - -

To a friend who's planning to date
a woman known as a man-killer,
you might say . . .

*Careful is the naked man climbin' a
barbwire fence.*

Antique Appraisal

Two young country girls meet for coffee one Saturday morning. "How was your blind date?" Raylene asks Betty Jo.

"Awful!" Betty Jo answers. "He showed up in a 1956 Ford pickup."

"The truck is a classic. What's so bad about that?"

Betty Jo sighs and explains, "He's the original owner."

Enchantment

- - - - - - - - -

To the person you've fallen for after
a couple of dates, you might say . . .

*Are your legs tired, 'cause you've been
runnin' through my dreams.*

Scoundrel

- - - - - - - - -

In advising a gal who's wondering
if she should go out with a fellow
who has a reputation as a cad,
you might say . . .

*It don't take no genius to spot a goat in a
flock of sheep.*

Spendthrift

- - - - - - - - -

Warning a friend who tries to
impress his woman by showering
her with jewelry, you might say . . .

*Broke is what happens when you let your
yearnin's get ahead of your earnin's.*

Age

- - - - - - - - -

To those wondering why a
gal would be dating someone much
older than her, you might say . . .

The old pipe gives the sweetest smoke.

The Perfect Companion

At the church social, a young woman tells her friend about her idea of the perfect mate: "The fellow I marry must be a shinin' light. He must be musical, tell jokes, sing, and stay home at night."

Overhearing the conversation, the old church lady pipes up, "Sugar, if that's all you want, get a TV."

Uncertainty

- - - - - - - - -

In advising a friend who is
concerned that he's falling for a girl
and isn't sure what to do about it,
you might say . . .

Ride the horse in the direction it's goin'.

Perseverance

- - - - - - - - -

To a woman who's losing faith that
she will ever fall for the right man,
you might say . . .

*You have to kiss a lot of toads before you
find your prince.*

Character

- - - - - - - - -

When describing a date with
a genuine, polite, trustworthy guy,
you might say . . .

He's a true copper-bottomed gentleman.

Suspicion

- - - - - - - - -

As a warning to a fellow
whose girlfriend works with his
good-looking, womanizing brother,
you might say . . .

*You can't trust your dog to watch your
food.*

Since You Asked . . .

After a minor tiff, Joe Don tells his girlfriend Priscilla, "I don't know how God could have made you so stupid yet so beautiful."

"I'd be tickled to explain," says Priscilla. "God made me beautiful so you would be attracted to me. God made me stupid so I would be attracted to you."

Fatal Attraction

Laura Beth and Dicky Ray went on a blind date that was a disaster from the start. No chemistry, no compatibility, no meaningful conversation. Earlier, Laura Beth had secretly arranged to have a friend call her at the diner so she would have an excuse to leave if something like this happened.

To her relief, the friend phoned the eatery and Laura Beth took the call. When she returned to the table, she dabbed her eyes and told Dicky Ray, "I have some bad news. My grandfather just died."

"Thank heavens," Dicky Ray replied. "If yours hadn't, mine would have had to."

Jeopardy

Advising someone who is
planning on dating a person known
to create havoc with the heart,
you might say . . .

*You can't keep trouble from comin', but
you don't have to give it a chair to sit on.*

Cruising

If you and your buddies are
looking for girls to go out with,
you might say . . .

Let's go sparrow catchin'.

Impression
- - - - - - - - -

In describing a fellow who's going
all out to make a big hit with a
young woman, you might say . . .

He's tryin' to make a mash on that girl.

Delusion
- - - - - - - - -

To a gal who's deceiving herself
into thinking that she'll be asked
out by a guy who everyone knows
is in love with someone else,
you might say . . .

You're flyin' away with the fairies.

17

Rejection

- - - - - - - -

To a guy who has been turned
down time and again for a date with
a certain girl, you might say . . .

You're barkin' at a knot.

Uncertainty

- - - - - - - -

If you're talking to a gal who's
not so sure about her feelings
for her once-hot boyfriend,
you might say . . .

*You didn't fall in love; you just
tripped over it.*

Late Night

After waiting at the restaurant
for more than an hour and a half
for her date, Mary Sue figured
she had been stood up. She went
home, slipped into her pajamas and
slippers, fixed a bowl of popcorn,
and began watching a rerun of *Hee
Haw*.

No sooner had she plopped
down in front of the TV when her
doorbell rang. There stood her date,
Elmer. He took one look at her and
gasped, "Gosh and tarnation! I'm
two hours late . . . and you still
ain't ready?"

Gaffe

- - - - - - - -

To a friend who realized she
had accidentally made dates with
two guys for the same night,
you might say . . .

You're in one all-fired bad box.

Rendezvous

- - - - - - - -

Speaking about being asked on
a date by the most eligible bachelor
in town, you might say . . .

*I'm steppin' out with the biggest toad
in the pond.*

Bad Judgment

- - - - - - - -

About a gal who constantly goes
out with the wrong guys,
you might say . . .

*She don't make mistakes.
She just dates 'em.*

Personality

- - - - - - - -

In describing the allure of a
recent date, you might say . . .

*She could charm the dew right off
the honeysuckle.*

Attraction

- - - - - - - - -

Talking about a fellow you're
smitten with, you might say . . .

*Every time I'm with him, I get more
butterflies than a field full of petunias.*

Frustration

- - - - - - - - -

If you've dated lots of women
without finding the right one,
you might say . . .

*I sowed wild oats and reaped prunes
and bran.*

Appearance

- - - - - - - -

Advising a gal who's concerned
that the nice guy she's dating isn't
very handsome, you might say . . .

A good horse is never a bad color.

Brashness

- - - - - - - -

To a fellow who always comes on
much too strong to the women he
meets, you might say . . .

A lasso ain't no datin' tool.

Free Spirit
- - - - - - - - -

Talking about the madcap girl
you're dating who follows the
beat of a different drummer,
you might say . . .

Oh, lordy, is she a caution!

Prudence
- - - - - - - - -

Warning a friend who's infatuated
with someone with a questionable
reputation, you might say . . .

*If you've fallen in love at first sight,
you better look twice.*

Attraction

- - - - - - - - -

In seeing a sexy woman flirt with
your buddy, you might say . . .

*She's battin' her eyes at you like a toad
in a hailstorm.*

Good Guy

- - - - - - - - -

If you're talking about the
nice guy you dated last night,
you might say . . .

There are few weevils in his cotton.

Honest-to-Goodness Real Country Songs

She Feels Like a New Man Tonight

♥ ♥ ♥

The Last Word in Lonesome
Is "Me"

♥ ♥ ♥

How Can You Believe Me When
I Say I Love You, When You Know
I've Been a Liar All My Life?

♥ ♥ ♥

All the Guys Who Turn Me On
Turn Me Down

♥ ♥ ♥

How Come Your Dog Don't Bite
Nobody But Me?

♥ ♥ ♥

High Cost of Low Living

♥ ♥ ♥

Run for the Roundhouse, Nellie
(He Can't Corner You There)

♥ ♥ ♥

If You Don't Believe I Love You
(Ask My Wife)

♥ ♥ ♥

She's Looking Better Every Beer

♥ ♥ ♥

My Shoes Keep Walking
Back to You

♥ ♥ ♥

If My Nose Was Running Money,
Honey (I'd Blow It All on You)

♥ ♥ ♥

I'll Dance at Your Wedding
(If You'll Marry Me)

Sex

- - - - - - - -

Advising a fellow who views
his dates as sex objects,
you might say . . .

*All that comes from a cow
ain't just milk.*

Cause and Effect

- - - - - - - -

If your friend complains that
every guy she goes out with is a
loser, you might say . . .

When you plant taters, you get taters.

Improbability

Talking about an uncouth, unemployed fellow who plans to ask the town beauty out on a date, you might say . . .

He has no more chance than a grasshopper in a chicken house.

Slut

In describing a woman with a bad reputation, you might say . . .

Men pass her around like a mess of corn bread.

Womanizer

- - - - - - - -

If you're warning your friend
against going out with a slick,
smooth-talking Lothario,
you might say . . .

*The devil can quote scripture
for his own ends.*

Appearance

- - - - - - - -

To those who wonder why
a good-looking guy is dating a
plain-looking gal, you might say . . .

*The eyes ain't responsible
for what the heart sees.*

Excuse

- - - - - - - -

If your date stood you up and
then came up with a cockamamie
reason why he couldn't call you
ahead of time, you might say . . .

*Your excuse is as weak as
day-old dishwater.*

Misfortune

- - - - - - - -

Talking about a fellow who keeps
striking out in the dating game,
you might say . . .

*He's gettin' nothin' but warm beer
and cold kisses.*

Good Date
- - - - - - - - -

In describing how much you
enjoyed a date that went better than
expected, you might say . . .

It was too fine for nice,
but it was great for good.

Immaturity
- - - - - - - - -

If you're talking about the
twenty-something you're dating
who still acts like a teenager,
you might say . . .

He's between hay and grass.

Attentiveness

- - - - - - - -

To those who wonder why an average-looking guy gets dates with the most sought-after girls, you might say . . .

The fragrance always stays on the hand that gives the rose.

Attraction

- - - - - - - -

Of a man who is smitten by a certain woman, you might say . . .

He's taken a shine to her.

Closeness

- - - - - - - - -

Talking about a couple who are always together, you might say . . .

Them two are as thick as hair on a dog's back.

Gentility

- - - - - - - - -

In describing how classy your date was, you might say . . .

He was a gentleman of the first water.

Solicitude

- - - - - - - -

In complaining about a gal who
is incredibly nice to the point of
excess, you might say . . .

She's so sweet she's givin' me a toothache.

Appeal

- - - - - - - -

To a guy you really like but are
playing coy with, you might say . . .

If you rope me, you can have me.

Allure

In describing a woman who is doing all she can to win the affections of a certain man, you might say . . .

She's set her cap for him.

Enchantment

Talking about someone who's fallen fast and hard after a few dates, you might say . . .

It's plain as the tail on a rattler that she's sweet on him.

Infatuation

If you're falling in love with
your sweetie pie, you might say . . .

I'm soft down on you.

Happiness

If you're head-over-heels in love,
you might say . . .

*If I were any peachier,
I'd be a cobbler.*

Fear

- - - - - - - - -

To a friend who's too afraid to
tell his sweetheart that he's in love
with her, you might say . . .

*You ain't got a hair on your butt
if you don't tell her.*

Poetry

- - - - - - - - -

To a friend who wants to recite
his gal a love poem that he wrote,
you might say . . .

*It's like a haircut—good, and you feel
like a million bucks; bad, and you hide
your head under your hat.*

Enchantment

- - - - - - - - -

About a couple who are madly
in love, you might say . . .

*Their hearts are a-poppin' like
the flowers in May.*

Coziness

- - - - - - - - -

If you're snuggled in the arms
of your sweetheart,
you might say . . .

*I'm as comfy as an egg under a
hen sittin' in a wool basket.*

My, How Times Change

Newlywed Betty Lou was sitting in the chair at the beauty parlor having her hair done and chattering happily about her new hubby. "He's everything I could hope for," she gushed. Then she rattled off a mess of good traits.

Violet, the beautician, who was on her third stormy marriage, cleared her throat and said, "Funny thing about new husbands. The same qualities that attracted you to him in the first place are usually the very ones you can't stand a year later."

Appearance

- - - - - - - -

To people wondering how a
beauty queen could fall in love
with a less than handsome man,
you might say . . .

Love is a great beautifier.

Absence

- - - - - - - -

If you're apart from your honey
for an extended period,
you might say . . .

*Life without you is like a
rosebush without flowers.*

Goofiness

- - - - - - - - -

If you're talking about a gal who's acting silly because she's smitten, you might say . . .

Ain't no cure for a girl in love.

Closeness

- - - - - - - - -

Talking about a lovey-dovey twosome who snuggle everywhere they go, you might say . . .

Now there goes a couple that's hip to haunch and cheek to jowl.

Long-Term Effect

Dixie woke up during the night to find her husband, Luke, wasn't in bed. She put on her robe, went downstairs, and found him sitting at the kitchen table with a double shot of moonshine in front of him. He was staring at the wall, wiping a tear from his eye.

"Why are you down here at this time of night, Luke?" she asked. "What's the matter?"

"Do you recollect twenty years ago when you were only sixteen and I was courtin' you?" he asked.

"Sure I do," she replied.

"And do you recollect that night your father caught us in the back of my pickup doin' the bump and grind?"

"Of course."

"Then you recollect him shovin' his shotgun in my face and yellin', 'Either you marry my daughter or spend the next twenty years in jail'?"

Dixie nodded.

Luke wiped another tear from his cheek and whined, "I would have been released today."

Fear

To a guy who's afraid to tell his
girlfriend how much he loves her,
you might say . . .

*You ain't never gonna break a horse if
you stay sittin' on the fence.*

Love

- - - - - - - - -

If you want to tell your
sweetie pie how much you're
in love, you might say . . .

*I love you more than a cat
loves the cream jar.*

♥ ♥ ♥

*Sure as corn bread goes with greens,
you're the answer to my dreams.*

♥ ♥ ♥

You make me happier than a pig in slop.

♥ ♥ ♥

*Sure as shootin', sure as hell,
you're the flowers in my dell.*

♥ ♥ ♥

A hundred wagons can't haul
all the love I have for you.

♥ ♥ ♥

You make me happier
than a gopher in soft dirt.

♥ ♥ ♥

Sure as vines wind 'round the stump,
you're my darlin' sugar lump.

♥ ♥ ♥

Baby doll, I wouldn't trade you
for a fatted cow.

*If I could reach the stars
I'd pull one down for you.*

*Sure as rain clouds come in June,
you're the heavens, stars, and moon.*

♥ ♥ ♥

I made a wish and you came true.

In your arms is my favorite place to be.

♥ ♥ ♥

Sure as creeks go 'round the bend,
my love for you knows no end.

♥ ♥ ♥

Earth ain't so bad 'cause
I'm in heaven with you.

♥ ♥ ♥

You're it as far as I can see.

♥ ♥ ♥

You're the onliest person who holds
the key that can open my heart.

♥ ♥ ♥

Sure as lightnin' goes with thunder,
without you I'd go asunder.

52

*If I had a single flower for every time
I think about you, I'd get lost in
my garden.*

You're the butter on my biscuit.

*Sure as God made all this land,
you hold my heart in your hand.*

*Lovin' you is like drinkin' hot cider —
it makes me feel warm all over.*

Loveliness

- - - - - - - - -

If you want to tell your
sugarplum how fetching she is,
you might say . . .

*You're prettier than a
blue-ribbon lamb on fair day.*

*You're as pretty as a spotted horse
in a pasture full of daisies.*

♥ ♥ ♥

*Sure as taters grow in dirt,
you look sexy in my shirt.*

*If I had a nickel for every time I saw a
gal as pretty as you, I'd have a nickel.*

You're as lovely as crimson and clover.

♥ ♥ ♥

You're sweeter than mama's tea.

♥ ♥ ♥

You're cuter than a babe in a blanket.

♥ ♥ ♥

*Sure as flowers bloom in spring,
you are such a pretty thing.*

*You're cuter than a heifer calf
in a pansy patch.*

Hell on Earth

Late one night, Ruth Ann came home from a date with her boyfriend. Her crestfallen face was streaked with tears.

"You look as gloomy as a treed coon," said her mama. "What's wrong, darlin'?"

"Billy-Ray proposed to me tonight," Ruth Ann replied.

"Well, hush my mouth!" her mama shouted with joy. "Ain't that the bee's knees! So why the long wet face?"

"He don't believe there's a hell."

"Marry him anyway," advised her mama. "Between the two of us, we'll show him just how wrong he is."

Proposal

- - - - - - - - -

If you're hinting at marriage,
you might say . . .

*We might could rest our heads
every night on the same pillow.*

♥ ♥ ♥

*Won't you ride with me down
Honeymoon Lane?*

*I'm a-yearnin' to add a branch
to your family tree.*

*You're the gal I want to
row down the river with.*

♥ ♥ ♥

*Let's lock our hearts together
and throw away the key.*

59

GETTIN' HITCHED

(Musin's 'bout Weddin's)

Happy Groom

- - - - - - - - -

In describing the happy groom,
you might say . . .

*He was grinnin' like a
skunk eatin' cabbage.*

Food for Thought

A traveling dietician stops in an Appalachian hollow to discuss with the local hill people the importance of good nutrition. "Most of you here have eaten entirely too many fried foods high in fat and empty calories," she informs them. "Can anyone tell me the most dangerous food of all?"

Cletus raises his hand and answers, "Weddin' cake."

Happy Daze

At the rehearsal dinner, the groom-to-be's Uncle Bill walks up to him and says, "Congratulations, boy. You'll look back on this day and remember it as the happiest day of your life."

"But, Uncle Bill, I ain't gettin' hitched 'til tomorrow," his nephew says.

Replies Uncle Bill, "I know, boy, I know."

Cold Feet

- - - - - - - - -

To a friend who's getting cold feet
an hour before the wedding,
you might say . . .

*When you're on a horse gallopin' off
a cliff, it's too late to shout "Whoa!"*

Sweet Ceremony

- - - - - - - - -

If you believe the old wives' tale
that an exceptionally sweet
wedding ceremony leads to an
exceptionally sweet marriage,
you might say . . .

A fine beginnin' makes a dandy endin'.

Reception Blessing

- - - - - - - - -

At the church hall supper after
the wedding, you might say . . .

*Bless the bride, bless the bowl,
bless the biscuits, give 'em soul.*

Questionable Choice

- - - - - - - - -

About a woman who married a
man most people didn't approve of,
you might say . . .

*That butterfly flew 'round all the pretty
flowers and landed on a cow pie.*

Cold Feet

- - - - - - - - -

To a friend who's getting cold feet
the night before the wedding,
you might say . . .

*Courage is bein' scared to death and
saddlin' up anyway.*

Good Fortune

- - - - - - - - -

Talking about the working class
groom who just married into a
wealthy family, you might say . . .

*He's got it made in the shade,
if the tree don't fall.*

Love for Sale

During the wedding rehearsal,
Bevis the groom approached the
preacher with an unusual offer:
"I'll give you one hundred bucks if
you'll change the weddin' vows."

"What do you want me to do?"
the preacher asked.

"When you get to the part where
I'm supposed to promise to love,
honor, obey, and be faithful to her
forever, just leave that part out."

The preacher took the bribe.

The next day at the ceremony,
it came time for the groom's vows.
The preacher looked Bevis in the
eye and said, "Will you promise to
prostrate yourself before her, obey
her every command and wish, serve

her breakfast in bed every morning, and swear eternally before God and your lovely wife that you will not even look at another woman for as long as you both shall live?"

Stunned speechless, Bevis gulped and looked around. All eyes were on him. Feeling totally betrayed and too afraid to bolt from the altar, he squeaked out, "I will."

When the ceremony was over, the groom, whose shock had turned to anger, pulled the preacher aside and, through clenched teeth, hissed, "I thought we had a deal."

"We did," admitted the preacher. Returning the $100 that Bevis had given him the day before, the preacher whispered, "But the bride made me a better offer."

Sweet Ceremony

- - - - - - - - -

In describing what a loving
and emotional wedding it was,
you might say . . .

It'd bring a tear to a glass eye.

Cold Feet

- - - - - - - - -

To a friend who's worried about
going through with the wedding,
you might say . . .

A faint heart never filled a flush.

Beautiful Bride

- - - - - - - - -

About a beautiful bride,
you might say . . .

*Grace was in her steps,
heaven in her eyes.*

Happy Groom

- - - - - - - - -

If you're a happy groom,
you might say . . .

*I'm plumb tickled to death to be walkin'
down the aisle of love.*

Amazing Ceremony

- - - - - - - - -

If you're enjoying the best
wedding you've ever attended,
you might say . . .

*I've been to three county fairs and
a hog butcherin' but I ain't never
seen nothin' like this before.*

Happy Newlywed

- - - - - - - - -

As you happily walk together out
of the church on your wedding day,
you might say . . .

*I've got the world by the tail
with a downhill pull.*

Wedding Sympathy

- - - - - - - - -

When seeing the groom walk
into the church, you might say . . .

*Well, that's the last real decision
he'll ever make.*

Like Father, Like Son-in-Law

At the wedding, Jenny couldn't help but notice that her friend Rita, the mother of the bride, was sobbing throughout the entire ceremony.

Later as the reception was winding down and the newlyweds had left, Jenny went over to comfort Rita, whose cheeks were still wet from tears. Jenny told her, "You're not losin' a daughter, you're gainin' a son. I had a chat with the groom and he reminds me so much of your husband. You know what they say: Girls tend to marry men who are like their fathers."

"I know," wailed Rita. "That's why I'm cryin'."

Old Wives' Tales
- - - - - - - - -

*Vows sweetly spoken won't ever
be broken.*

♥ ♥ ♥

A lovely day, a lovely bride.

♥ ♥ ♥

*A weepin' bride will be a
laughin' wife.*

♥ ♥ ♥

*A laughin' bride will be a
weepin' wife.*

♥ ♥ ♥

Marry in May, rue the day.

76

♥ ♥ ♥

Marry in white, always be right.

♥ ♥ ♥

Marry in blue, always be true.

♥ ♥ ♥

Marry in brown, live in town.

♥ ♥ ♥

Marry in black, don't look back.

♥ ♥ ♥

Marry in green, never be seen.

♥ ♥ ♥

Marry in red, wish you were dead.

WEARIN' THE YOKE

(Hoots an' Hollers 'bout Marriage)

Different Woman

- - - - - - - - -

To a friend who complains that his wife isn't the same person he had married, you might say . . .

Trouble with a milk cow is she won't stay milked.

Big Trouble

- - - - - - - - -

In advising your buddy who's about to be in big trouble with his wife because he was out late drinking with you, you might say . . .

When it's your butt that's about to go for a ride, try havin' more common sense than pride.

Fair Trade

Old Man Grady was dying, so his family stood around his deathbed and tried to comfort the farmer in his final hours. In a weary voice, he whispered to his wife, Darlene, "After I've left for the hereafter, I want you to marry Wade, the farmer over in the next county."

"No, I can't marry anyone after you," she protested.

"Dadgummit, woman, I insist!" he wheezed.

Perplexed, Darlene asked, "But why?"

With his final breath, Grady replied, "He cheated me in a horse trade."

Body of Evidence

Darryl's wife, Jo-Dee, was the jealous type. When he came home after a night of drinking with the boys, she carefully examined his jacket, looking for strands of a woman's hair. When she couldn't find any, she pitched a hissy fit anyway: "So now you're cheatin' on me with a bald-headed woman!"

The next night, Darryl went out again. When he returned, Jo-Dee sniffed him from head to toe, but she couldn't find any trace of perfume on him. Nevertheless, Jo-Dee had another conniption: "She's not only bald-headed, but she's too cheap to buy perfume!"

Solid Marriage

- - - - - - - -

If you're describing an enviable
relationship, you might say . . .

*Their marriage is as strong
as a pine knot.*

Bad Moment

- - - - - - - -

To a friend in a solid,
loving marriage who confided
that he and his wife had a spat,
you might say . . .

Well, every day ain't Sunday.

Happy Home

- - - - - - - - -

A sign over the door of a
happy home might say . . .

Forever thine, forever mine, forever ours.

Milquetoast Hubby

- - - - - - - - -

Talking about a husband who
doesn't stand up to his harping wife,
you might say . . .

*Woe to the house where the hen crows
and the rooster keeps still.*

Misplaced Interest

- - - - - - - - -

To a married friend who spends
way too much time on his hobby,
you might say . . .

*Never give your horse more
attention than your wife, unless you
like sleepin' in the barn.*

Intimate Bond

- - - - - - - - -

In describing a marriage where
the couple is secure in their
relationship, you might say . . .

*Their bond is as comfy as a garden
hammock in the summer shade.*

Roaming Husband

- - - - - - - - -

If you're offering advice to a friend whose husband is always seen carousing without her, you might say . . .

A loose horse is always lookin' for new pastures.

Tumultuous Twosome

- - - - - - - - -

In talking about a passionate couple that acts madly in love one moment and shouts madly in anger the next, you might say . . .

Their marriage might have been made in heaven, but so are thunder and lightnin'.

Good Fortune

- - - - - - - -

When explaining how you've
remained married for so long,
you might say . . .

*We've stayed hitched all these years
by guess and by God.*

Control Issues

- - - - - - - -

Advising a friend whose
husband makes all the decisions,
you might say . . .

*Just 'cause you're followin' a
well-marked trail don't mean that
whoever made it knows where he's goin'.*

Side Effects

Conway had been slipping in and out of a coma for several months, yet his devoted wife, Scarlett, stayed by his bedside every single day.

When he finally regained consciousness, he motioned for her to sit on his bed. As he held her hand, Conway said, "You've been with me through all the bad times. When I fell off the barn roof and broke my leg, you were there. When the tractor ran over me, you were there. When the farm failed, you were there. When we lost the house, you were there. Now my health is failin', yet you're still by my side."

Scarlett was leaning in to give him a kiss when he added, "I'm beginnin' to think you're bad luck!"

Gloomy Twosome

- - - - - - - - -

In describing an unhappy couple,
you might say . . .

*That marriage is all
beer and skittles.*

Anger Management

- - - - - - - - -

In revealing one of the secrets
to a successful marriage,
you might say . . .

Don't let the moon see your wrath.

Tough Decision

- - - - - - - - -

Advising a stay-at-home mom
who is wondering whether to leave
her husband, you might say . . .

*Never take to sawin' on the branch
that's supportin' you, unless you're
bein' hung from it.*

Rough Patches

- - - - - - - - -

As a reminder that every
marriage has its bad moments,
you might say . . .

*There never is a lane so long
that it don't have some hills and curves.*

What's Not to Like?

While Caleb and Dolly are weeding the garden, they get into a little cuss fight.

"You hate my mama; just admit it," Dolly snaps. "You hate all my kin."

"That ain't true," Caleb says. "In fact, I like your mother-in-law a whole lot better than I like mine."

Unexplained Attraction

- - - - - - - - -

Of someone who remains married to a jerk who's loud and obnoxious, you might say . . .

There's no accountin' for taste, as the ol' woman said when she kissed the cow.

Control Issues

- - - - - - - - -

To an overbearing and demanding friend who's wondering why his wife is threatening to leave him, you might say . . .

You're drivin' your mule too hard.

Intimate Bond

- - - - - - - - -

Talking about a married couple
who think and act alike,
you might say . . .

*They're like two volumes
of the same book.*

Bad Moments

- - - - - - - - -

If you hit a few rough patches
in an otherwise good marriage,
you might say . . .

*Sometimes the better comes
after the worse.*

Happy Marriage

- - - - - - - - -

If you're celebrating an anniversary
that's reached double digits, you
might want to tell your spouse . . .

Sure as water flows down hill,
kissin' you is still a thrill.

Marital Acrimony

- - - - - - - - -

If you're fed up with your
husband, you might say . . .

All men are idiots, and I married
their king.

Mirror, Mirror on the Wall . . .

Wynonna and her husband, Clayton, were getting ready for bed when she stood in front of their full-length mirror and examined her appearance for a spell. She shook her head and muttered, "I look in the mirror and see an old woman. My face is all wrinkled, my hair is gray, my shoulders are hunched over, I've got fat legs, and my arms are flabby."

She turned to her husband and pleaded, "Clayton, please tell me something positive to make me feel better about myself."

Clayton stared at her for a moment and then, in a thoughtful voice, said, "Pumpkin, there ain't nothin' wrong with your eyesight."

A Cure Worse Than the Disease

Pearl drove her ailing husband, Jethro, to the doctor's office in the next county. After the checkup, the doctor called Pearl into his office to speak to her alone.

"Your husband is suffering from a very severe stress disorder," the doctor explained. "If you don't follow my instructions to the letter, he won't live much longer. Every morning, fix him a big breakfast. Bake him a pie to serve at supper. Be pleasant at all times. Don't burden him with chores. Don't discuss your problems with him and, most important, don't nag him. It will only make his stress worse. If you can do this for the next year, I think your husband might regain his health completely."

On their way home, Jethro asked Pearl, "So what did the doctor say?"

Pearl shook her head and replied, "He said you was gonna die."

Reassuring Words

- - - - - - - -

To your spouse who's worried
about the future, you might say . . .

If the sky falls, we'll catch larks.

Assertive Woman

- - - - - - - -

When referring to a marriage in
which the wife rules the roost,
you might say . . .

*Now that there's a house run
by a petticoat government.*

Static Marriage

- - - - - - - - -

In describing a relationship in
which neither partner has grown,
you might say . . .

*That marriage is like yesterday's
corn bread—stale and dry.*

Marital Diplomacy

- - - - - - - - -

In explaining why you
cave in to your wife,
you might say . . .

*No use in me arguin' with her,
'cause it's like bringin' a knife
to a gunfight.*

Long Time Comin'

While enjoying an early morning breakfast in a small-town café, four elderly farmers jawed on subjects such as cattle, horses, the weather, and the good old days.

Eventually the conversation focused on their spouses. One of the farmers turned to his friend on the right and asked, "Buford, ain't you and the missus fixin' to celebrate your fiftieth weddin' anniversary soon?"

"Yup, we sure are," Buford replied.

"Are you gonna do something special to celebrate?" another farmer asked.

After swallowing a forkful of biscuits and gravy, Buford replied, "Well, for our fortieth anniversary, I took Bea to visit her sister over in Possum Hollow. Maybe for our fiftieth, I'll go down there and get her."

Anger Management

- - - - - - - - - -

If your friend confides that he's
angry at his wife, you might say . . .

*Don't feel bad about thinkin' ill of her,
'cause she's probably thought
worse 'bout you.*

Tumultuous Twosome

- - - - - - - - - -

About a couple who are always
arguing, you might say . . .

There go blood and thunder.

Assertive Woman

- - - - - - - - -

A sign over the door of a quiet
home might say . . .

*My wife submits and I obey;
she always lets me have her way.*

Marital Bribery

- - - - - - - - -

To an abusive husband who
buys his wife nice things after
each one of his transgressions,
you might say . . .

*Money will buy a fine dog, but only
kindness will make him wag his tail.*

It's All Relative

During a physical exam, the doctor told Orville, "It's odd for a strapping young lad like you to have such high blood pressure."

"It comes from my kin, Doc," said Orville.

"I've been taking care of your family for years, and there's never been a history of high blood pressure," the doctor countered.

"It don't come from my side of the family," Orville replied. "It comes from my wife's side."

"Oh, balderdash," the doctor said. "You can't get high blood pressure from your wife's side of the family."

Orville sighed and explained, "You haven't met my in-laws."

Critical Spouse

- - - - - - - -

To your carping spouse,
you might say . . .

*I feel like a banjo 'cause you're
always pickin' on me.*

Happy Marriage

- - - - - - - -

If you're celebrating an anniversary,
you might tell your spouse . . .

*Sure as squirrels live in trees,
I'm for you and you're for me.*

Housebroken

All the employees of the town's biggest and most successful cotton mill were married men.

When a strong-willed woman went to apply for a job there, she was turned down flat. Confronting the manager, she said, "Why do you hire only married men? Is it because you think women are weak, dumb, and cantankerous?"

"Not at all, Missy," the manager replied. "It's because married men are used to obeyin' orders, gettin' shoved around, keepin' their mouths shut, and not poutin' when they get yelled at."

The Last Word

Chester and his much younger friend Boyd were sitting out in front of the feed store playing checkers when Boyd asked, "How long have you been married?"

After some thought, Chester answered, "Pert near fifty years now, I reckon."

"Woo-ee!" Boyd exclaimed. "What's the secret?"

Chester leaned back in his chair and replied, "I always get in the last word whenever we kick up a ruckus."

"How do you manage that?" asked Boyd.

Answered Chester, "I tell her, 'Yes, Honey!'"

Marital Freedom

- - - - - - - -

As a reminder to your spouse
that each needs a bit of space,
you might say . . .

A loose rein keeps the marriage tight.

Aging Couple

- - - - - - - -

When talking to your spouse
about growing old together,
you might say . . .

*We're like a couple of prunes.
As time goes by, we're gettin' wrinkled,
but a whole lot sweeter.*

Mad Money

After Russell carried his bride, Sara Jane, across the threshold of their first house, she placed a shoe box on a shelf in her closet and asked him never to touch it.

For fifty years Russell left the box alone. But one day, while he was searching for the deed to his pickup, he spotted the box. Caving in to temptation, he opened it. To his surprise, he found two doilies and $75,000 in cash. He put the box back in the closet.

Puzzled about what he had found, he confessed to Sara Jane

that he had opened the box and begged her to explain the contents.

"Mama gave me that box the day you and I got hitched," Sara Jane explained. "She told me to make a doily for every time that I got mad at you." Russell was genuinely touched that in a half century, his wife had been mad at him only twice. "So where did the $75,000 come from?" he asked.

"Oh," replied Sara Jane, "that's the money I made from selling the rest of the doilies."

Foolish Argument

After a knock-down, drag-out, barn-burner of an argument, Bubba snarls at his wife, "Dadgummit, Betty Sue, I was a fool when I married you."

Betty Sue rubs her hands on her apron and replies, "I know, Bubba. But I was in love back then and didn't notice."

Marital Diplomacy

- - - - - - - - -

If you want to agree with your wife,
you might say . . .

Whatever blows your dress up.

Reassuring Calm

- - - - - - - - -

If your spouse cheers you up
after a tough day, you might tell
your sweetie . . .

*You give me comfort like sunshine
after rain.*

Bad Moments

- - - - - - - - -

As a reminder to your spouse not to
focus too much on the unpleasant
moments of an otherwise good
marriage, you might say . . .

*Count the orchard by the fruit it bears
and never by the leaves that fall.*

Happy Marriage

- - - - - - - - -

If you're celebrating an anniversary,
you might tell your spouse . . .

*Sure as young 'uns always ask why,
you are the apple of my eye.*

Honest-to-Goodness Real Country Songs

You're the Hangnail in My Life,
and I Can't Bite You Off

♥ ♥ ♥

You're the Reason Our
Kids Are So Ugly

♥ ♥ ♥

I Went Back to My Fourth Wife
for the Third Time and Gave
Her a Second Chance to Make
a First-Class Fool Out of Me

♥ ♥ ♥

If You Want Your Freedom PDQ,
Divorce Me COD

♥ ♥ ♥

This White Circle on My Finger
Means We're Through

♥ ♥ ♥

You Ain't Much Fun
Since I Quit Drinkin'

♥ ♥ ♥

You're a Hard Dog
to Keep Under the Porch

♥ ♥ ♥

Don't Come Home A-Drinkin'
(With Lovin' on Your Mind)

♥ ♥ ♥

If I Had It to Do All Over Again,
I'd Do It All Over You

♥ ♥ ♥

Her Wedding Ring's a
One-Man Band

♥ ♥ ♥

I Wish I Had Died at the Altar

♥ ♥ ♥

I Wish I Had My First Wife Back

ROLLIN' IN THE HAY

(Look-Sees 'bout Sex)

Fish Tale

One Friday morning, Earl called home and told his wife, Leann, "Sugar Plum, the boss asked me to go on a fishin' trip with him and the other big shots for the weekend. Here's my chance to angle for that promotion you've been harpin' on me to get. Be an angel and pack up my clothes for the weekend and set out my rod and reel and tackle box. And don't forget to toss in my new blue pajamas. We're leavin' from the office so I'll swing by the house on the way out to pick up my things."

Leann's mind was swirling with suspicion but she did what she was told. A few hours later, Earl showed

122

up at home just long enough to grab his things and give his wife a peck on the cheek. Then he flew out the door.

Sunday night, Earl returned bushed but otherwise fine. Leann welcomed him back and asked, "Did you catch many fish?"

"Yep," Earl replied. "We caught a mess of catfish and bluegill and a few crappies. By the way, how come you didn't pack my new blue pajamas like I asked you?"

"I did," said Leann, reaching for her rolling pin. "They were in your tackle box."

Cohabitation

- - - - - - - - -

If people wonder why you and
your partner don't get married,
you might say . . .

*No reason to buy the cow
when you can get the milk for free.*

or

*No reason to buy the pig
when you can get the sausage for free.*

Frustration

- - - - - - - - -

To a friend who complains that he isn't getting enough loving from his sweetheart, you might say . . .

*If you ain't gettin' fed at home,
then go out to eat.*

Exhaustion

- - - - - - - - -

When you've had all the fun you can stand in bed, you might say . . .

I'm plumb tuckered out.

Some Things You Never Forget

An elderly couple, Sadie Mae and Floyd, were sitting in their rockers on the porch, watching the beautiful sunset. Sadie turned to Floyd and said, "Lamb Chop, do you recollect when we first started sparkin' and you'd hold my hand?"

Floyd glanced over at his wife, grinned, and obligingly took her aged hand in his.

Batting her eyes, Sadie said, "Do you recollect how after we were engaged, you'd kiss me on the cheek?"

Floyd leaned over to his wife and gave her a lingering smooch.

Sadie smiled and said, "Do you recollect how, after we were first married, you'd nibble on my ear and then we'd go do the hoochie-coochie?"

Floyd sprang from his rocker and hobbled as fast as he could into the house.

Surprised, Sadie asked, "Lamb Chop, where are you goin'?"

Floyd yelled back, "To get my teeth!"

Beefcake

If your friends marvel at your
lover's body, you might say . . .

He's as fit as a butcher's dog.

Cheating

When describing a tart who was
caught cheating on her husband,
you might say . . .

*She was larkin' about and
got her wings clipped.*

Lover

- - - - - - - - -

When asked to describe a
notorious lover, you might say . . .

He's as wild as a peach orchard hog.

Passion

- - - - - - - - -

If you want to have another round
in the sack with your lover, you
might say . . .

Let's keep the pot a-boilin'.

Quandary

To a friend who is wondering
if she should go home with the
cute guy she met at the party,
you might say . . .

*When you climb into the saddle,
you'd better be prepared to ride.*

Gentleness

In explaining to a friend
why it's important not to rush
things in bed with his girlfriend,
you might say . . .

The fastest way to move cattle is slowly.

Fling

- - - - - - - - -

If you're talking to someone
who's having an illicit affair,
you might say . . .

*What you do in the dark
will eventually come to light.*

Passion

- - - - - - - - -

If you want to keep the bedsprings
bouncing, you might say . . .

*Let's keep whoopin' it up
'til the cows come home.*

Skill

- - - - - - - - -

In describing an experienced lover,
you might say . . .

He sure knows his onions.

Sexist

If you're a sexist pig who thinks
women aren't worth dating unless
they put out, you might say . . .

Color don't count if the horse don't trot.

Ancestry

Talking about someone who was
born out of wedlock and doesn't
know her father, you might say . . .

*She was born on the wrong side
of the blanket.*

Seein' Is Believin'

Newlywed Ada Mae was getting plumb worn out by her husband, Farley's overactive sex drive. She finally confided to her minister who just happened to hold a psychology degree.

"I know your husband won't talk to me about this situation, but I have a plan," said the minister. He handed Ada Mae several numbered pages, each with a different ink blot on it. "Show these to your husband and write down what he says about each one," he instructed. "Then come back here and I'll try to figure out what the problem might be."

Later after dinner, Ada Mae brought out the ink blots. She held up the first one and asked Farley, "Dumplin', what do you see?"

He studied the ink blot for a moment and said, "That's a man and a woman havin' relations."

Showing him the next ink blot, she asked, "What's this a picture of?"

"A man and a woman havin' relations," Farley replied.

Ada Mae held up the third ink blot. "And what do you see here?"

"A man and a woman havin' relations."

Upset and frustrated, Ada Mae flung the rest of the ink blots onto the floor and declared, "You're just obsessed with sex!"

"Me?" Farley countered. "That ain't hardly fair. You're the one who keeps showin' me the dirty pictures!"

Waitin' for the Right Time

About midnight, a sheriff's deputy drives up to Lovers' Lane and recognizes a car belonging to his twenty-five-year-old cousin Hardy, the county's sleaziest womanizer. The deputy walks up to the car. To his surprise, he sees Hardy reading a book in the front seat and a sexy girl knitting in the back.

The deputy says, "Hardy, what are you two doin'?"

"Nothin' bad," Hardy replies. "I'm readin' and she's knittin'."

The cop turns to the girl and says, "You look mighty young. How old are you?"

She checks her watch and answers, "I'll be eighteen in 'bout five minutes."

Mistake

- - - - - - - -

If your friend is moaning the
morning after that she had sex with
someone she wished she hadn't,
you might say . . .

Well, the corn is off the cob.

Passion

- - - - - - - -

If you hear a couple who are a
little too loud in their lovemaking,
you might say . . .

*They're makin' more noise than a
couple of jackasses in a tin barn.*

Appeal

- - - - - - - - -

If you're ogling a sexy young thing,
you might say . . .

*I wouldn't kick her out of bed for eatin'
soda crackers.*

Exhaustion

- - - - - - - - -

When you've had all the fun
you can stand in bed for the night,
you might say . . .

Stick a fork in my buns 'cause I'm done.

A Question of Lust

After an all-nighter of passion, the young man whispers to his bride-to-be, "Sugar Lips, am I the first man to make love to you?"

"Of course you are, pumpkin," she says. Then she rolls her eyes and adds, "I don't know why you men always ask me the same ridiculous question."

Sex

- - - - - - - -

As a way of suggesting the two
of you hop in the sack,
you might say . . .

Let's talk less and say more.

Rear

- - - - - - - -

When talking about your
sweetheart's bare behind,
you might say . . .

*The first time I laid hands on your
Sunday face, I gave a prayer of thanks.*

Premarital Relations

- - - - - - - - -

Talking about a couple who had
a child a few months after they
married, you might say . . .

*The young 'un didn't come early;
the weddin' came late.*

Skill

- - - - - - - - -

In giving advice to a friend on
making whoopee, you might say . . .

Fast is fine, but good is better.

Contentment

- - - - - - - - -

If your lover asks how you feel
after a wild night of passion,
you might say . . .

*I'm slightly burned out,
but I'm still smokin'.*

Secret

- - - - - - - - -

As a warning to someone who is
trying to keep an illicit affair secret,
you might say . . .

It'll all come out in the wash.

Saving Up for Marriage

For all his born days, seventy-year-old Otis had been a bachelor. But then he courted a twenty-five-year-old gold digger who agreed to marry him only after he told her he had been saving up for over fifty years.

After returning from their two-week honeymoon in the Bahamas, they attended a church social. With a big smile, a jaunty step and a twinkle in his eyes, Otis told his friends that getting married was the best thing he'd ever done. "I didn't see much of the sea or sun, if you get my drift," he boasted.

On the other side of the gathering, his young bride appeared dog tired and right haggard. "Lord have mercy!" exclaimed her friend. "You told me that after marryin' that old geezer you'd have it made in the shade. But you look like you've been run through the mill for a week and twice on Sunday. What happened?"

"Otis double-crossed me," the gold digger complained. "He told me he had saved up for over fifty years . . . and I thought he was talkin' about money!"

Passion

If you still have time for another
roll in the hay before you have to
go to work, you might say . . .

*Don't stop kickin' 'til the
clock stops tickin'.*

Appeal

If you're ogling a hunk of
burning love, you might say . . .

*He can put his boots
under my bed anytime.*

Slut

- - - - - - - -

Talking about a woman who doesn't
know who the father of her unborn
baby is, you might say . . .

*She ran through a patch of briars and
don't know which one stuck her.*

Cheating

- - - - - - - -

To someone who is fooling around
on his wife, you might say . . .

*You're gonna end up suppin' sorrow
with a long spoon.*

Passion

Talking about the night you and
your sweetie were making love with
wild abandon, you might say . . .

We were goin' at it like killin' snakes.

Honest-to-Goodness Real Country Songs

I May Be Used
(But Baby, I Ain't Used Up)

♥ ♥ ♥

Do You Love
as Good as You Look?

♥ ♥ ♥

I'll Marry You Tomorrow
but Let's Honeymoon Tonight

♥ ♥ ♥

She Offered Her Honor,
He Honored Her Offer, and
All through the Night It
Was Honor and Offer

♥ ♥ ♥

Get Your Biscuits in the Oven
and Your Buns in the Bed

♥ ♥ ♥

Thanks to the Cathouse,
I'm in the Doghouse with You

♥ ♥ ♥

You Done Me Wrong,
But at Least You Done Me

♥ ♥ ♥

It Don't Feel Like Sinnin' to Me

♥ ♥ ♥

Heaven's Just a Sin Away

♥ ♥ ♥

Going to Hell in Your
Heavenly Arms

♥ ♥ ♥

(I Can't Take Your Body)
If Your Heart's Not in It

♥ ♥ ♥

Now I Lay Me Down to Cheat

♥ ♥ ♥

If You Can't Be Good,
Be Bad with Me

♥ ♥ ♥

If You're Gonna Do Me Wrong,
Do It Right

♥ ♥ ♥

It Ain't Easy Being Easy

♥ ♥ ♥

This Good Girl's Gonna Go Bad

♥ ♥ ♥

Make Me Late for Work Today

♥ ♥ ♥

I Never Went to Bed
with an Ugly Woman
(But I Sure Woke Up with a Few)

♥ ♥ ♥

Think of Me
(When You're Under Him)

PARTIN' WAYS

(Digs an' Cuts 'bout Breakin' Up)

Cast Off

- - - - - - - - -

In describing how you got jilted by your girlfriend, you might say . . .

She flicked me off like a spent match.

Rejection

- - - - - - - - -

When talking about a woman who had turned down a beau's proposal and then booted him out of her life, you might say . . .

She sure gave him the mitten.

Put-Down

- - - - - - - - -

If you're splitting from your
boyfriend after he did you wrong,
you might say . . .

*I wouldn't poke air holes in the top of a
pickle jar if you were stuck inside.*

Clash

- - - - - - - - -

In describing a rather loud
breakup argument at a restaurant,
you might say . . .

They went at it hammer and tongs.

Unsecured Loan

Loretta went to the bank to apply for a loan. "I want to borrow enough money to divorce my husband," she told the bank manager.

"Sorry, but we don't give loans for divorces" he said, "We make loans for appliances, automobiles, businesses, home improvements. . . ."

Loretta interrupted him and said, "Well, fine then. This certainly qualifies as a home improvement."

Shortcomings

- - - - - - - - -

If there are more drawbacks
than benefits to sticking with a
relationship, you might say . . .

*I'd just as soon do without the eggs
as to hear her cackle.*

Cold Shoulder

- - - - - - - - -

In describing the silent treatment
you received from your
girlfriend when you broke up,
you might say . . .

She wouldn't say pea turkey squat to me.

Breakup Advice

- - - - - - - - -

To a pal who's planning to
break up with his girlfriend,
you might say . . .

*Speak your mind,
but ride a fast horse.*

Divorce

- - - - - - - - -

If you're talking about a couple who
got divorced, you might say . . .

She put him on the porch.

Put-Down

- - - - - - - -

If you're splitting from your
sweetheart after she did you wrong,
you might say . . .

I wouldn't pee on you if you were on fire.

Second Thoughts

- - - - - - - -

About someone you pursued and
caught, but then realized you really
didn't want, you might say . . .

*I guess my eyes were bigger
than my heart.*

Pay Pal

"Mr. Bodine, I've reviewed the case very carefully," the divorce court judge says, "and I've decided to give your wife $275 a week."

"That'll work, Your Honor," Bodine concurs. "And every now and then I'll try to send her a few bucks myself."

Consequences

- - - - - - - - -

If your spouse left you because you were unfaithful, you might say . . .

I had her leavin' comin'.

Cast Off

- - - - - - - - -

Talking about a guy who was unceremoniously dumped by his girlfriend, you might say . . .

Oh, lordy, did he sit down on a bear trap.

Threat

- - - - - - - - -

To a friend who wants to threaten
her boyfriend that she'll leave him
even though she really wouldn't,
you might say . . .

If you can't bite, don't growl.

Heartache

- - - - - - - - -

About someone who just got
dumped and is taking it hard,
you might say . . .

He'll be drinkin' his Christmas dinner.

Change

- - - - - - - -

To a gal who split with her
boyfriend after she failed to change
his wild behavior, you might say . . .

You can't shoe a runnin' horse.

Put-Down

- - - - - - - -

If you're breaking up because
your partner was too cold
and aloof, you might say . . .

*You're as tender as a
hangin' judge's heart.*

Music to the Ears

Jesse called up his ex-wife, Trisha, and, while disguising his voice, asked, "Can I speak to Jesse, please?"

"Sorry, he don't live here no more," she answered. "We're divorced."

The next day, Jesse did the same thing and got the same answer. In fact, he called Trisha every day for a week until finally his ex-wife realized who was on the other end of the line. "Hey, you boil-brained weasel, we ain't married no more," Trisha railed. "When are you gonna get that through your fat head? We're divorced!"

"Oh, I know," Jesse responded calmly. "I just like hearing you say it."

Callousness

- - - - - - - - -

About a girl who treated her
boyfriend badly before dumping
him, you might say . . .

*She walked across his heart
like it was Texas.*

Glare

- - - - - - - - -

If your girlfriend gave you the evil
eye after you suggested dating other
people, you might say . . .

She looked mighty blue at me.

You Have the Right to Remain Silent

On the way home from the barn dance, Jake and his wife, Daisy, were cussing out each other in their pickup. The two were so all-fired up that it turned into a barn-burner — one that eventually turned their marriage into ashes.

Here's what happened: At the height of their donnybrook, Jake was pulled over by a policeman. The officer explained that he had stopped Jake because his taillight was burned out.

"I'm sorry, Officer," Jake said politely. "I didn't know it was out. I'll fix it right away."

But then Daisy piped up, "I knew this would happen. Jake, I told you two weeks ago to get that taillight fixed."

The officer frowned and asked for Jake's driver's license. After studying it, the cop said, "Sir, your license has expired."

Jake apologized profusely. "I didn't realize that, Officer. I promise to take care of it first thing in the morning."

Daisy let out a sarcastic laugh and said to Jake, "I told you a month ago that your license had expired and you wouldn't do anything about it."

By this time, Jake was getting a might ill with Daisy for contradicting him in front of the policeman. Losing his temper, Jake snapped, "Daisy, shut your cotton-pickin' trap!"

The officer leaned toward Daisy and asked, "Ma'am, does your husband always talk to you like that?"

Daisy replied smugly, "Only when he's drunk."

Consequences

About a guy whose sweet and loving wife finally divorced him because he kept straying from his marriage, you might say . . .

He just pissed in his whiskey.

Wrath

Talking about a wife who threw her husband out after he came home late and drunk for the umpteenth time, you might say . . .

She was as mad as a calf with a barbwire tail.

Heartache

- - - - - - - - -

To a friend who's been pining
away for days over a lost love,
you might say . . .

Don't just lay there and bleed.

Breakup Advice

- - - - - - - - -

To a friend who wants to dump her
lover because she's got her eyes on
another guy, you might say . . .

*Don't throw away the old bucket 'til you
know whether the new one holds water.*

173

No Return Policy

At the square dance, Mary Lou goes over to Lacy Jane and whispers, "I hear tell you broke off your engagement to Calvin. What happened?"

"It's just that my feelin's toward him ain't the same anymore," Lacy Jane replies.

"Are you fixin' to give back the ring?"

"Heavens, no!" says Lacy Jane. "My feelin's toward the ring haven't changed one iota."

Vexation

In explaining why you split from
your girlfriend, you might say . . .

*She was so exasperatin'
she could make a preacher cuss.*

Cheater

If you caught your lover cheating
on you, you might say . . .

*You must have been hidin' behind the
door when they were passin' out morals.*

Abuser
- - - - - - - - -

If you're leaving your abusive lover,
you might say . . .

*I'd rather jump barefoot off a six-foot
stepladder into a five-gallon bucket
full of porcupines than spend
another night with you.*

Spendthrift
- - - - - - - - -

If you're splitting up with your
boyfriend because he's so cheap,
you might say . . .

*You're as tight as a hawk's butt
in a nosedive.*

Rage

- - - - - - - - -

In describing to your friends
later how angry you were at him
when he broke up with you,
you might say . . .

I sure gave 'em down the country!

Heartbreak

- - - - - - - - -

If you're still sad over your recent
breakup, you might say . . .

I've had the blue devils all week.

A Failure to Communicate

Earnest the farmer walked into the country lawyer's office and announced, "I want to get one of them divorces."

The lawyer said, "Do you have any grounds?"

"Yep, I got about one hundred forty acres."

The lawyer chuckled and said, "You don't understand. Do you have a case?"

"No, I ain't got no Case. I got a John Deere."

Feeling a touch of frustration, the lawyer asked, "I mean do you have a grudge?"

"Yep, I got a grudge. That's where I park my Case."

The lawyer tried to remain calm, but it wasn't easy. He decided to try a different line of questioning. "Do you have a suit?"

"Yep. I wear it to church on Sundays."

The lawyer took a deep breath and, holding his irritation in check, asked, "Well, does your wife beat you up?"

"Nope. We both get up the same time."

Finally, in exasperation, the lawyer bellowed, "Why in God's green earth do you want a divorce?"

Earnest replied, "I can't never have a meanin'ful conversation with her."

Vexation

If you can't convince your
sweetheart that he's making a huge
mistake in suggesting you date
other people, you might say . . .

*If you can't change your mind,
are you sure you have one?*

Cheater

To a guy who has been unfaithful
to you, you might say . . .

You can cheat a fish out of its scales.

180

Jerk

If you're breaking up with a guy
who pretends to be a gentleman but
is really an arrogant, egotistical cad,
you might say . . .

You're nothin' but a barber's clerk.

Heartache

Seeing the sad look on a friend
who got dumped, you might say . . .

*You have a face as long as
a Missouri mule.*

Divorce Advice

- - - - - - - - -

If your divorced friend asks
what he should do with his old
wedding ring, you might say . . .

*Ain't no need for pockets
on a dead man's coat.*

Rage

- - - - - - - - -

To the guy who angered you so
much that you dumped him on
the spot, you might say . . .

Go boil your shirt!

Incompatibility
- - - - - - - - -

In explaining why you're
splitting with your lover because
neither of you gets along anymore,
you might say . . .

The two of us just can't seem to gee-haw.

Put-Down
- - - - - - - - -

To your ex-lover, you might say . . .

*You are the raspberry seed
between my teeth.*

Oppression

If you're breaking up because your
partner has been smothering you
to death, you might say . . .

Love can't grow in the shade.

Liar

If you're splitting up with
someone who lies all the time,
you might say . . .

*I'm ditchin' your sorry behind 'cause
you're too tight with the truth.*

For Love
or Money

Dear Sweet Pea,

I've been so down in the mouth ever since I broke off our engagement. I was dead wrong. I must have been touched in the head. Won't you please offer forgiveness and come back to me? You hold a cherished place in my heart that no other woman will ever touch. We were made for each other like biscuits and gravy. I love you so.

Yours forever and ever,
Buck

P.S. Congratulations on winning the million-dollar lottery!

185

Nit-Picker

- - - - - - - - -

To the woman you're dumping
because you can't take her
incessant carping any longer,
you might say . . .

*You'd complain if your ice cream were
cold and hell weren't hot enough.*

Cheater

- - - - - - - - -

If you're splitting from your man
because he cheated on you, you
might say . . .

You hurt the love right out of me.

Heartache
- - - - - - - - -

If your loved one is thinking
of breaking up with you,
you might say . . .

*Good-bye ain't painful unless you ain't
plannin' on sayin' hello again.*

Fury
- - - - - - - - -

In describing how loud the girl was
swearing at her boyfriend during
their breakup, you might say . . .

Oh, was she airin' out her lungs.

Tenacity

If you're not ready to quit
a relationship even though
your partner already has,
you might say . . .

*Don't forget me 'cause if you do,
I ain't leavin'.*

Cheater

To the cad you're breaking up with
because he went out with your
best friend, you might say . . .

*You're so low you could walk under a
snake without bendin' your knees.*

Critic

To the lover you're dumping
because he's always criticizing you,
you might say . . .

Love don't keep no lists of wrongs.

Heartache

If you got your heart broken when
you got jilted, you might say . . .

She struck a match to the book of love.

Divorce Advice

- - - - - - - - -

In offering support to a friend who's
wondering if she should go through
with a divorce, you might say . . .

*Go ahead and choke the horn
and claw the leather.*

Honest-to-Goodness Real Country Songs

You Changed Your Name from Brown to Jones, and Mine from Brown to Blue

♥ ♥ ♥

How Can I Miss You If You Won't Go Away?

♥ ♥ ♥

She Got the Gold Mine and I Got the Shaft

♥ ♥ ♥

My Wife Ran Off with My Best Friend, and I Sure Do Miss Him

♥ ♥ ♥

Thank God and Greyhound
She's Gone

♥ ♥ ♥

If You Don't Leave Me Alone
(I'll Find Someone Else Who Will)

♥ ♥ ♥

I Was Looking Back to See if
You Were Looking Back to See if
I Was Looking Back to See if You
Were Looking Back at Me

♥ ♥ ♥

Get Your Tongue Outta My Mouth
'Cause I'm Kissin' You Good-bye

♥ ♥ ♥

All My Exes Live in Texas

♥ ♥ ♥

If the Phone Don't Ring, It's Me

♥ ♥ ♥

If You Can't Live Without Me,
Why Aren't You Dead?

♥ ♥ ♥

She Made Toothpicks from
the Timber of My Heart

♥ ♥ ♥

If Fingerprints Showed Up
on Skin, Wonder Whose I'd
Find on You

♥ ♥ ♥

I Keep Forgettin' I Forgot
About You

♥ ♥ ♥

I Don't Know Whether to
Kill Myself or Go Bowling

♥ ♥ ♥

I'm So Miserable Without You
(It's Almost Like You're Here)

♥ ♥ ♥

Billy Broke My Heart at Walgreens
and I Cried All the Way to Sears

♥ ♥ ♥

I Bought the Shoes That Just
Walked Out on Me

♥ ♥ ♥

If Drinkin' Don't Kill Me,
Her Memory Will

♥ ♥ ♥

All I Want from You (Is Away)

♥ ♥ ♥

Feelin' Single and Drinkin' Doubles

♥ ♥ ♥

Here's a Quarter
(Call Someone Who Cares)

♥ ♥ ♥

Flushed You from the
Toilets of My Heart

♥ ♥ ♥

My Lips Want to Stay
(But My Heart Wants to Go)

♥ ♥ ♥

Which Way Do I Go
(Now That I'm Gone)?

♥ ♥ ♥

Drinking to Forget What
I'm Drinking to Forget

♥ ♥ ♥

I Can't Get Over You 'til
You Get Out from Under Him

♥ ♥ ♥

I Miss You Already
(And You're Not Even Gone)

♥ ♥ ♥

I Need Somebody Bad Tonight
('Cause I Just Lost Somebody
Good)

♥ ♥ ♥

I've Got Tears in My Ears from
Lyin' on My Back in Bed and
Cryin' on My Pillow Over You

♥ ♥ ♥

She Got the Green
and I Got the Blues

♥ ♥ ♥

When You Leave, Walk Out
Backwards So I'll Think
You're Walking In

♥ ♥ ♥

You're the Reason
I'm Not Over You

♥ ♥ ♥

If You Leave Me, Can I Come Too?

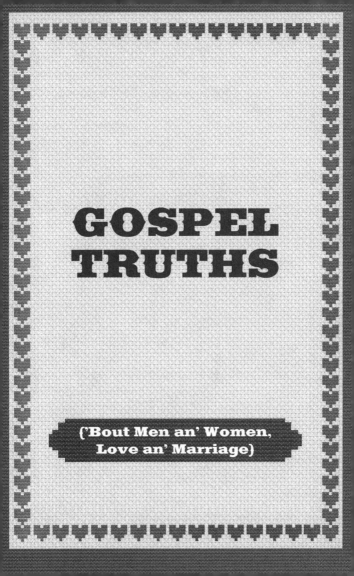

GOSPEL TRUTHS

('Bout Men an' Women, Love an' Marriage)

Marriage

*If you don't have a sense of humor
in your marriage, you probably don't
have no sense at all.*

♥ ♥ ♥

*Work at havin' a good marriage.
That way, when you get older and look
back at your lives together, you'll enjoy
it a second time.*

♥ ♥ ♥

*Don't marry the man you can live with.
Marry the man you can't live without.*

♥ ♥ ♥

*Some women get excited
about nothin' . . . and then marry him.*

♥ ♥ ♥

*The best thing to hold on to in life
is each other.*

♥ ♥ ♥

*A house is built with boards
and beams . . . A home is built with
love and dreams*

♥ ♥ ♥

Happiness is home brewed.

♥ ♥ ♥

*Have love in your heart and
peace in your home.*

♥ ♥ ♥

*A happy home is the father's kingdom,
the mother's world, and the
child's paradise.*

The calmest husbands
make the stormiest wives.

♥ ♥ ♥

Never marry for money.
You can borrow it cheaper.

♥ ♥ ♥

More things belong to marriage
than four bare legs in a bed.

♥ ♥ ♥

A deaf husband and a blind wife
are always a happy couple.

♥ ♥ ♥

Marriage is a shortcut to a long life.

♥ ♥ ♥

A happy home is but an early heaven.

♥ ♥ ♥

No matter what, no matter where,
it's always home if love is there.

♥ ♥ ♥

Love ain't a matter of countin' the years.
What matters is makin' the years count.

♥ ♥ ♥

If love is blind, marriage is a
real eye-opener.

♥ ♥ ♥

Any married man should forget his
mistakes 'cause there ain't no use in two
people recollectin' the same things.

♥ ♥ ♥

Life's a voyage that's homeward bound.

♥ ♥ ♥

*A woman marries a man expectin'
he'll change, but he don't. A man
marries a woman expectin' she
won't change, but she does.*

♥ ♥ ♥

*There are two times when a man
don't understand a woman —
before marriage and after.*

♥ ♥ ♥

*If love is one long sweet dream,
marriage is the rooster's crow.*

♥ ♥ ♥

Memories are stitched with love.

♥ ♥ ♥

Have a heart that never hardens,
a temper that never tires,
and a touch that never hurts.

♥ ♥ ♥

Love and marriage go together
like grits and gravy.

Dating

- - - - - - - - -

*When it comes to datin', there are
more horses' asses than horses.*

Women

- - - - - - - - -

*Women come and go,
but your tools last forever.*

Men

- - - - - - - - -

*Men are like the weather.
Nothin' can be done to change 'em.*

Personal Experience

When Wanda Sue stood in the checkout line at the local Piggly Wiggly, she showed off her engagement ring to the cashier.

Zack, a grizzled good ol' boy with a six-pack under each arm, was next in line. He congratulated Wanda Sue and then offered her an observation about marriage. "The first ten years are the hardest," he said.

"How long have you been married?" Wanda Sue asked.

Replied Zack, "Ten years."

Anger

- - - - - - - - -

*An angry bull is less dangerous
than an angry woman.*

Spooning

- - - - - - - - -

*A man chases a woman
until she catches him.*

Sucker

- - - - - - - - -

Don't kiss a fool or let a kiss fool you.

Men

- - - - - - - - -

Men are like barbwire—
they have their bad points.

Quarrel

- - - - - - - - -

There are two beliefs about arguin' with
women, and neither one of 'em works.

Drinking

- - - - - - - - -

A smile from a good woman is worth
more than a dozen from a bartender.

Flour Girl

Bo and his wife, Roxanne, were attending a church gathering, listening intently to the minister talk about the need for communication in marriage.

"It is essential that husbands and wives know each other's likes and dislikes," the minister said. Turning to Bo, he asked, "Can you name your wife's favorite flower?"

Bo felt pretty confident in his answer. He leaned over, patted his wife's hand and said, "It's Pillsbury, ain't it, angel?"

Fool

- - - - - - - - -

Only a fool argues with a skunk,
a mule, or a wife who can cook.

Men

- - - - - - - - -

Men are like pears.
The older they are, the softer they get.

Priorities

- - - - - - - - -

The most important things a man can
get in this world are somethin' to eat,
somethin' to drink, and someone to love.

Deadly Demands

Dewey was a mild-mannered man who was tired of being bossed around by his wife, Marvella, so he went to his preacher to complain. The preacher said Dewey needed to build up his self-esteem and gave him a lecture on assertiveness. "You must tell her exactly what it is you want from her," the preacher told him.

After the session, Dewey was all fired up and stormed into the house. Pointing a finger in Marvella's face, he thundered, "From now on,

I am the man of this house, and my word is law! Tonight you will fix me country-fried steak with cherry cobbler. When I'm finished eatin', you're gonna draw me a nice, relaxin' bath. And when I'm finished with that, guess who's gonna dress me and comb my hair?"

With a stone face, Marvella replied, "The funeral director."

Precise Advice

Old Man Haywood was having a heart-to-heart with Kenny, a strapping young lad who was on the lookout for the right girl to marry.

"Son, take it from me," said Haywood. "There are four things every man should know when huntin' for a wife. One, find a woman who's good at household chores and can cook up a storm. Two, find a woman who loves to go dancin' and can hold her liquor. Three, find a woman who'll make whoopee with you anytime, anywhere."

"What's the fourth thing?" asked Kenny.

Replied Haywood, "It is very important that these three women never meet."

Understanding

- - - - - - - - -

*To be happy with a man, you need to
understand him a lot and love him
a little. To be happy with a woman,
you need to love her a lot and not
understand her at all.*

Quarrel

- - - - - - - - -

*A woman has the last word in any
argument. Anythin' a man says after
that is the beginnin' of a new argument.*

Men

- - - - - - - - -

*Women don't make fools of men
'cause most men can do it themselves.*

Honesty

- - - - - - - - -

*It's better to be hated for who you are
than loved for who you ain't.*

217

Love
- - - - - - - - -

*True love is when you're still dancin'
long after the music stopped.*

*Fallin' in love ain't so hard. It's like
strollin' through a pasture—sooner or
later you're gonna step in it.*

*Love puts the joy in bein' together
and the sadness in bein' apart.*

*Love is like wildflowers—
it blooms in the most unlikely places.*

♥ ♥ ♥

*Love is the reason two people sit in the
middle of the bench when there's
room on both ends.*

*Life with your sweetie don't have
to be perfect to be wonderful.*

♥ ♥ ♥

*Go after love as if it's somethin' that's got
to be roped in a hurry before it gets away.*

♥ ♥ ♥

*Makin' it in love is kind of like bustin'
broncos. You're gonna get thrown a lot.
The secret is to keep gettin' back on.*

Love ain't love 'til you give it away.

A true love stays when the rest of the world walks out.

Seeds of love always bloom with joy.

♥ ♥ ♥

It's easy to fall in love. The hard part is findin' someone to catch you.

Love is like checkers, except both sides win.

♥ ♥ ♥

A heart that loves is always young.

Live by the sun, love by the moon.

♥ ♥ ♥

Love is like kudzu—it spreads.

♥ ♥ ♥

*To feel rich, count all the things you
and your sweetheart have that
money can't buy.*

♥ ♥ ♥

*To love and be loved is to feel the sun
from both sides.*

About the Authors

Allan Zullo, who lives with his wife, Kathryn, on a mountain outside of Asheville, North Carolina, has penned nearly one hundred nonfiction books. For more information about Allan, go to www.allanzullo.com.

Gene Cheek, a native Carolinian who also lives near Asheville, is the author of the critically acclaimed memoir *The Color of Love*. For more information about Gene, go to www.genecheek.com.

We're continuing to collect country sayings for future books and for our annual boxed calendar *Butter My Butt and Call Me a Biscuit*, which is produced by Andrews McMeel Publishing, LLC, the same company that is publishing this book. (It also published our book *Butter My Butt and Call Me a Biscuit: And Other Country Sayings, Say-Sos, Hoots, and Hollers*.)

If you would like to share your favorite country sayings, send them to our Facebook page, Butter My Butt. If there's one we haven't heard before and we use it in our next book or calendar, we'll send you a free copy.